THE INTERMEDIATE INTERVENTION PROGRAM

Student Guide

Level 6

Senior Author
J. David Cooper

Authors
Irene Boschken
Janet McWilliams
Lynne Pistochini

HOUGHTON MIFFLIN

Boston • Atlanta • Dallas • Denver • Geneva, Illinois • Palo Alto • Princeton

Design, Production, and Illustration: PiperStudiosInc

2001 Impression

Printed in the U.S.A.

ISBN: 0-395-78134-5

13 14 15-WC-04 03 02 01 00

SOAR TO SUCCESS

Contents

Book 1 *Nana Hannah's Piano*
Reflections 5

Book 2 *The Story of Three Whales*
Reflections 8

Book 3 *The Secret Room*
Reflections 11

Book 4 *Ruth Law Thrills a Nation*
My Notes to Clarify 14
Reflections 15

Book 5 *Why Are Whales Vanishing?*
My Notes to Clarify 18
Reflections 19

Book 6 *Detective Donut and the Wild Goose Chase*
Story Map 21
My Notes to Clarify 22
Reflections 23

Book 7 *Sweet Dried Apples*
Story Map 25
My Notes to Clarify 26
Reflections 27

Book 8 *Wilma Unlimited*
Story Map 30
My Notes to Clarify 31
Reflections 32

Book 9 *Sea Turtles*
K-W-L Chart 35
My Notes to Clarify 36
Reflections 37

Book 10 *Paricutín*
Event Map 40
My Notes to Clarify 41
Reflections 42

SOAR TO **SUCCESS**

Book 11 *Fire on the Mountain*
Story Map 44
My Notes to Clarify 45
Reflections 46

Book 12 *Roberto Clemente*
Event Map 49
My Notes to Clarify 50
Reflections 51

Book 13 *Storms*
Main Idea and Details Chart 54
My Notes to Clarify 55
Reflections 56

Book 14 *Danger on Midnight River*
Story Map 59
My Notes to Clarify 60
Reflections 61

Book 15 *There's a Wolf in the Classroom*
K-W-L Chart 65
My Notes to Clarify 66
Reflections 67

Book 16 *Shoeshine Girl*
Story Map 71
My Notes to Clarify 72
Reflections 73

Book 17 *Mummies and Their Mysteries*
K-W-L Chart 77
My Notes to Clarify 78
Reflections 79

Book 18 *Windcatcher*
Story Map 83
My Notes to Clarify 84
Reflections 85

Strategy Prompts 89

Book Log 93

Name ______________________________

REFLECTION 1

How do you think Sonny felt after his piano teacher told him he was hopeless? Explain.

REFLECTION 2

Do you think Nana should have answered when Sonny said "I guess when it comes to music, you either have it or you don't"? Why or why not?

Name ____________________

REFLECTION

3

Why do you think Sonny wants to play a song for Nana Hannah?

___

___

___

___

___

___

Nana Hannah's Piano

Name ______________________________

REFLECTION

Circle the strategy you used most in *Nana Hannah's Piano*.

Strategy Box			
Predict	**Summarize**	**Clarify**	**Question**

Name at least one place where you used this strategy or modeled it for someone else. Write the page number(s).

____

____

____

____

How did this strategy help you?

____

____

____

____

____

____

____

Name ______________________

REFLECTION

1

Why do whales swim south in the winter?

____

____

____

REFLECTION

2

Why do you think the Inuit expected the whales to die?

____

____

____

____

____

____

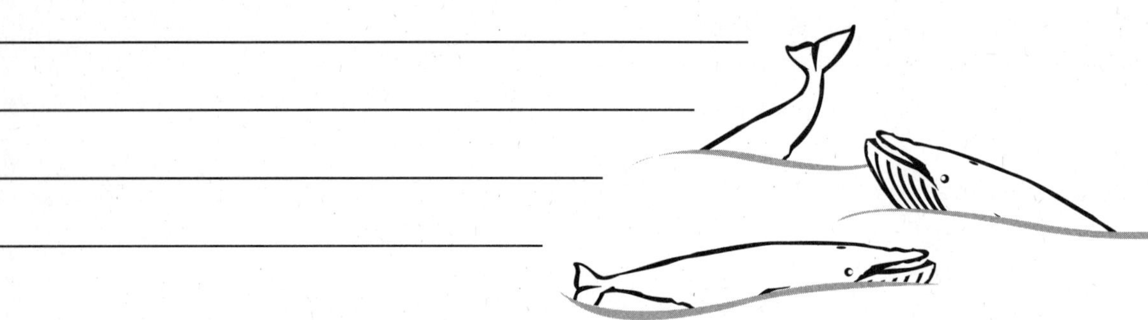

Name ______________________________

Circle a strategy that helped you.

Strategy Box			
Predict	**Summarize**	**Clarify**	**Question**

Name at least one place where you used this strategy or modeled it for someone else. Write the page number(s).

____

____

____

How did this strategy help you?

____

____

____

____

____

Name ______________________

REFLECTION

4

What did people learn from saving these whales?

Name ________________________________

REFLECTION

1

Do you think the old man's answer was clever? Explain.

REFLECTION

2

Why did the chief counselor ask the king's companion where they had traveled?

The Secret Room

Name ______________________

REFLECTION 3

Circle the strategy you used most.

Strategy Box			
Predict	**Summarize**	**Clarify**	**Question**

Name at least one place where you used this strategy. Write the page number(s).

____

____

How did this strategy help you?

____

____

____

____

Name ______________________________

REFLECTION

4

Do you think the man will make a good counselor to the king? Explain.

Name ______________________

My Notes to Clarify

Write any words or ideas that you need to clarify. Include the page numbers.

Words or Ideas	Page
Pages 4–13	
Pages 14–21	
Pages 22–32	

Name ______________________________

REFLECTION

1

Why did Ruth Law try to fly from Chicago to New York in one day?

____

____

____

____

____

What record would you yourself like to break? Explain your answer.

____

____

____

Ruth Law Thrills a Nation

Name ______________________________

REFLECTION

2

Was Ruth foolish to set out for New York without lights? Explain your answer.

Name ________________________________

REFLECTION 3

Circle a strategy that helped you read the story so far.

Strategy Box			
Predict	**Summarize**	**Clarify**	**Question**

How did this strategy help you?

____

____

____

____

____

Name ______________________

My Notes to Clarify

Write any words or ideas that you need to clarify. Include the page numbers.

Words or Ideas	Page
Pages 4–9	
Pages 10–17	
Pages 18–22	

Name ______________________________

REFLECTION

1

Why are whales such amazing creatures?

REFLECTION

2

Summarize why old-fashioned whaling methods didn't cut down the numbers of living whales.

Why Are Whales Vanishing?

Name ______________________________

REFLECTION 3

Circle the section you liked best in *Why Are Whales Vanishing?* Explain why you chose that section.

Pages 4–9
Exploring Our Environment
Amazing Creatures of the Depths
Whales with Teeth and Whales Without

Pages 10–17
Why People Have Hunted Whales
Whaling, the Old-fashioned Way
Whaling, the Modern Way
Oceans of Problems

Pages 18–22
Saving the Whales
How Can You Help?
Making the World Safe for Whales

____

____

____

How did one or more of the four strategies help you read that section?

Predict ______________________________

____

Summarize ______________________________

____

Clarify ______________________________

____

Question ______________________________

____

Name ______________________________

Story Map

Title

Setting

Characters

Problem

Major Events

Outcome

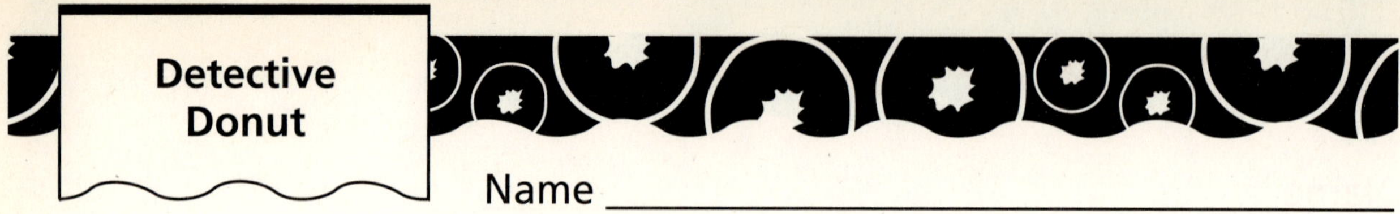

Name ___________________________

My Notes to Clarify

Write any words or ideas that you need to clarify. Include the page numbers.

Words or Ideas	Page
Pages 4–11	
Pages 12–17	
Pages 18–23	
Pages 24–27	
Pages 28–32	

Name ______________________________

REFLECTION

1

Think about what you know so far about Detective Donut. Then use three or four adjectives to describe him .

____

____

____

REFLECTION

2

On page 12, how does the author play with the meaning of break?

____

____

____

REFLECTION

3

Why is Donut easily tricked by the Professor's assistant?

____

____

____

Detective Donut

Name ______________________________

REFLECTION 4

Why doesn't Donut realize that Mouse is the one who caught the thief?

____

____

____

REFLECTION 5

Circle a strategy that helped you read *Detective Donut*.

Strategy Box			
Predict	**Summarize**	**Clarify**	**Question**

How did this strategy help you?

____

____

____

Name ______________________________

Story Map

Title

Setting

Characters

Problem

Major Events

Outcome

Name ____________________

My Notes to Clarify

Write any words or ideas that you need to clarify. Include the page numbers.

Words or Ideas	Page
Pages 5–11	
Pages 12–19	
Pages 20–27	
Pages 28–32	

Name ______________________________

REFLECTION

1

Duc and his sister often teased their grandfather. How do his reactions show what kind of a person he was?

REFLECTION

2

Tell about the two children's everyday life before the war.

Name ______________________

REFLECTION

3

Describe how you think the family felt hiding under the schoolroom.

What do you think they feared might happen?

Name ______________________________

REFLECTION

Circle the section you liked best in *Sweet Dried Apples*.

Pages 5–11
Ba goes to war; Ong Noi comes.

Pages 12–19
Ong Noi teaches the children and then leaves.

Pages 20–27
The sister and brother find and dry guava bits for Ong Noi. He returns and tells them to hide under the schoolroom. Then he dies.

Pages 28–32
Ma, Duc, and his sister, moving like shadows, leave the village and take a boat.

How did one or more of the four strategies help you read that section?

Predict

____

____

Clarify

____

____

Summarize

____

____

Question

____

____

Name ______________________________

Story Map

Title

Setting

Characters

Problem

Major Events

Outcome

Name ______________________________

My Notes to Clarify

Write any words or ideas that you need to clarify. Include the page numbers.

Words or Ideas	Page
Pages 8–13	
Pages 14–19	
Pages 20–27	
Pages 28–33	
Pages 34–43	

Wilma Unlimited

Name ______________________________

REFLECTION 1

Summarize what happened to Wilma as a young girl.

____

____

____

____

REFLECTION 2

How does Wilma feel as she sits and watches her classmates play?

____

____

____

____

Name ______________________________

REFLECTION

3

Why do you think Wilma was able to walk without her brace?

REFLECTION

4

Why did Wilma's chances of winning at the Olympics seem limited?

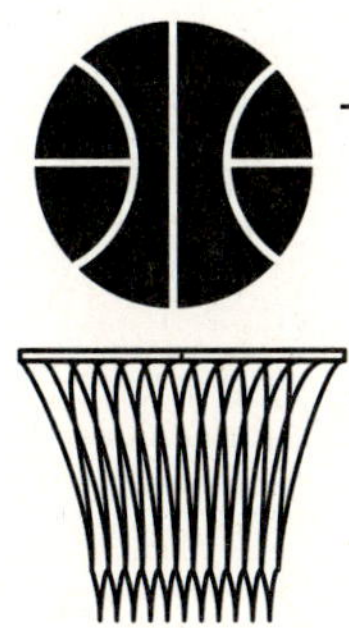

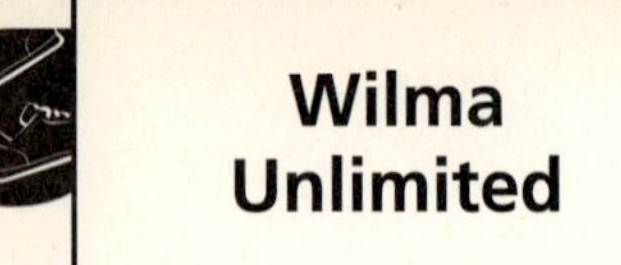

Name ______________________________

Circle the section you liked best in *Wilma Unlimited.*

Pages 8–13	**Pages 14–19**	**Pages 20–27**	**Pages 28–33**	**Pages 34–43**
Wilma gets sick.	Wilma works at her exercises.	Wilma begins to walk, and gets rid of her brace.	Wilma plays basketball, and goes to the Olympics.	Wilma wins gold medals for three races.

How did one or more of the four strategies help you read that section?

Predict

____

____

Clarify

____

____

Question

____

____

Summarize

____

____

Name ______________________________

K-W-L Chart

Title

What I **K**now	What I **W**ant to Find Out	What I **L**earned

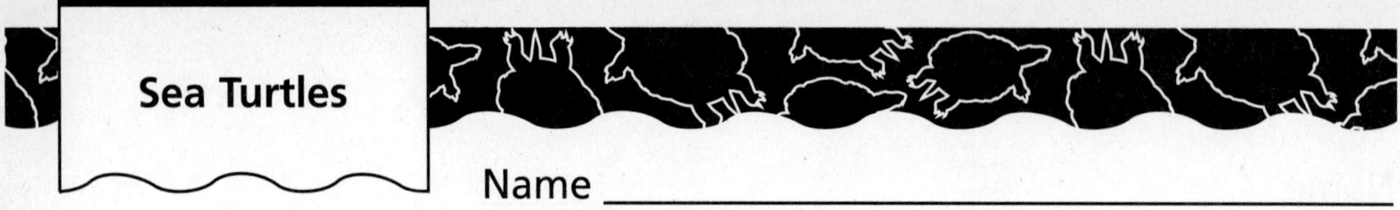

Sea Turtles

Name ______________________

My Notes to Clarify

Write any words or ideas that you need to clarify. Include the page numbers.

Words or Ideas	Page
Pages 4–11	
Pages 12–15	
Pages 16–25	
Pages 26–31	
Pages 32–37	
Pages 38–43	

Name ____________________________________

REFLECTION

1

How did land turtles become sea turtles long ago?

____

____

____

____

____

REFLECTION

2

What do the five kinds of U.S. sea turtles have in common?

____

____

____

____

Name ____________________

REFLECTION

3

Summarize how a sea turtle nests.

REFLECTION

Why do you think some baby sea turtles move away from the sea instead of toward it?

Name ______________________________

REFLECTION 5

Why does a sea turtle migrate?

____

____

____

____

REFLECTION 6

Circle a strategy that was helpful with this book.

Strategy Box			
Predict	**Summarize**	**Clarify**	**Question**

Explain how you used this strategy.

____

____

____

____

Name ______________________________

Event Map

Title
Event 1
Event 2
Event 3
Event 4
Event 5
Event 6
Event 7
Event 8

Name ______________________________

My Notes to Clarify

Write any words or ideas that you need to clarify. Include the page numbers.

Words or Ideas	Page
Pages 3–11	
Pages 12–21	
Pages 22–30	

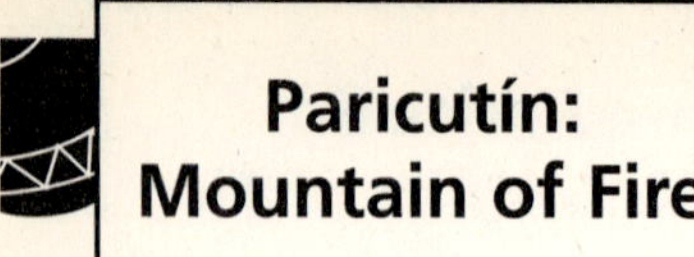

Paricutín: Mountain of Fire

Name ______________________

REFLECTION

1

How is Pablo's life different than yours? How is it similar?

____

____

____

____

REFLECTION

2

Circle the section you liked best so far in *Paricutín: Mountain of Fire.*

Pages 3–11	**Pages 12–21**
The town festival	The volcano appears; the townspeople react.

How did one or more of the four strategies help you read that section?

Predict ______________________

____

Clarify ______________________

____

Summarize ______________________

____

Question ______________________

____

Name ______________________________

REFLECTION

3

Use your Event Map to write a summary of the story.

Name ______________________________

Story Map

Title

Setting

Characters

Problem

Major Events

Outcome

Name ______________________________

My Notes to Clarify

Write any words or ideas that you need to clarify. Include the page numbers.

Words or Ideas	Page
Pages 6–13	
Pages 14–21	
Pages 22–27	
Pages 28–34	

Fire on the Mountain

Name ______________________

REFLECTION 1

How do you feel about what has happened to Alemayu so far?

____

____

____

____

____

REFLECTION 2

How do you think Alemayu's sister feels as Alemayu goes into the mountains?

____

____

____

____

____

Name ________________________________

REFLECTION

3

How did Alemayu survive the cold night in the mountains?

____

____

____

____

____

____

Do you think that people in real life can help themselves by imagining things? Explain your answer.

____

____

____

____

Name ____________________

REFLECTION

Choose a strategy that was helpful for reading *Fire on the Mountain.*

Strategy Box			
Predict	**Summarize**	**Clarify**	**Question**

How did this strategy help?

____

____

____

____

____

Name ______________________________

Event Map

Title

Event 1

Event 2

Event 3

Event 4

Event 5

Event 6

Event 7

Event 8

Name ______________________________

My Notes to Clarify

Write any words or ideas that you need to clarify. Include the page numbers.

Words or Ideas	Page
Pages 1–8	
Pages 9–20	
Pages 21–27	
Pages 28–40	
Pages 41–45	
Pages 46–53	

Name ______________________________

REFLECTION 1

Why did Roberto feel good after moving the pile of sand?

REFLECTION 2

Why did Roberto throw the javelin on the track team?

Name ______________________

REFLECTION

3

Summarize how Roberto got to be a Pittsburgh Pirate.

REFLECTION

4

How do you think Roberto felt when he was treated unfairly as a Spanish speaker?

Name ______________________________

REFLECTION **5**

Circle the strategy you used the most while reading *Roberto Clemente.*

Strategy Box			
Predict	Summarize	Clarify	Question

How did this strategy help you?

____

____

____

____

____

REFLECTION **6**

How did Roberto try to help the people of Managua?

____

____

____

____

____

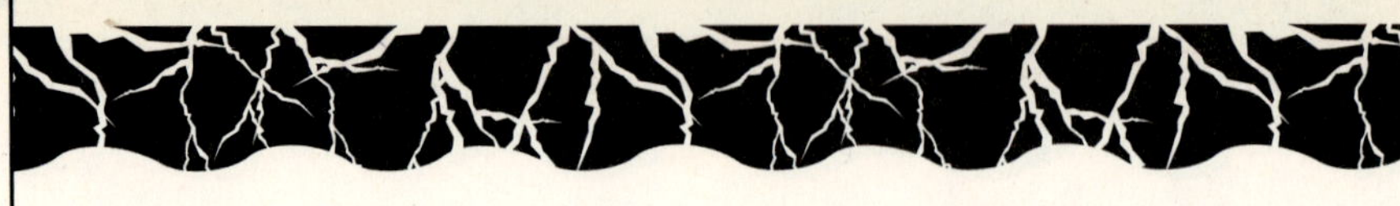

Name ______________________________

Main Ideas and Details

Title ______________________________

1. Main idea ______________________________

a. Detail ______________________________

b. ______________________________

c. ______________________________

d. ______________________________

2. ______________________________

a. ______________________________

b. ______________________________

c. ______________________________

d. ______________________________

3. ______________________________

a. ______________________________

b. ______________________________

c. ______________________________

d. ______________________________

4. ______________________________

a. ______________________________

b. ______________________________

c. ______________________________

d. ______________________________

Name ______________________________

My Notes to Clarify

Write any words or ideas that you need to clarify. Include the page number.

Words or Ideas	Page
Pages 4–11	
Pages 12–21	
Pages 22–27	
Pages 28–32	

Storms

Name ______________________

REFLECTION 1

How do air and water work together to form a thunderstorm?

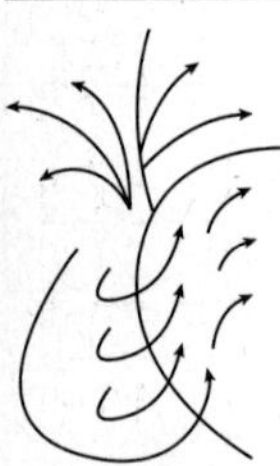

REFLECTION 2

The author writes about several ways storms can cause damage. Describe some of them.

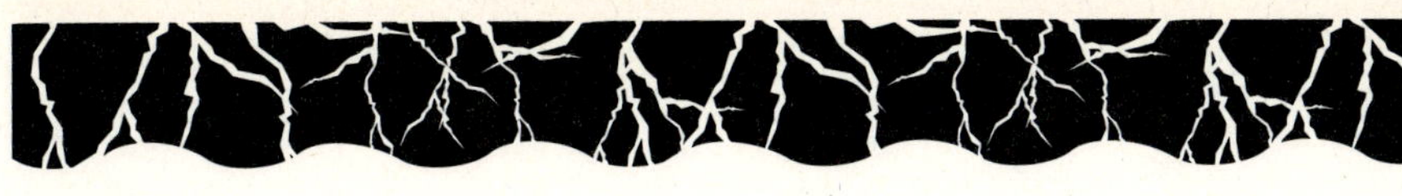

Name ____________________________________

REFLECTION 3

Which strategies have you used while reading *Storms?*

____

Explain how and why each strategy helped you.

Predict

____

____

____

Question

____

____

____

Clarify

____

____

____

Summarize

____

____

____

Name ______________________

REFLECTION

4

Suppose you want a friend to read this book. What facts from the book would you share to catch his or her interest?

Name ______________________________

Story Map

Title

Setting

Characters

Problem

Major Events

Outcome

Name ______________________________

My Notes to Clarify

Write any words or ideas that you need to clarify. Include the page number.

Words or Ideas	Page
Pages 1–7	
Pages 9–18	
Pages 19–31	
Pages 33–41	
Pages 43–55	
Pages 57–65	

Name ______________________________

REFLECTION 1

Why would Daniel rather be with his uncle than with boys his own age?

REFLECTION 2

If you were in Daniel's place, would you have helped the other boys? Why or why not?

Name ______________________________

REFLECTION

3

Do you think Scotty, Troy, and Brandon are wise to go their own way? Why or why not?

____

____

____

____

____

____

REFLECTION

4

Describe what Daniel is like as a person. What are his strengths and weaknesses?

____

____

____

____

____

____

Name ___________________________________

Circle one of the strategies you used.

Strategy Box			
Predict	**Summarize**	**Clarify**	**Question**

Name at least one place where you used this strategy. Write the page number(s).

____

____

____

____

How did this strategy help you?

____

____

____

____

____

____

____

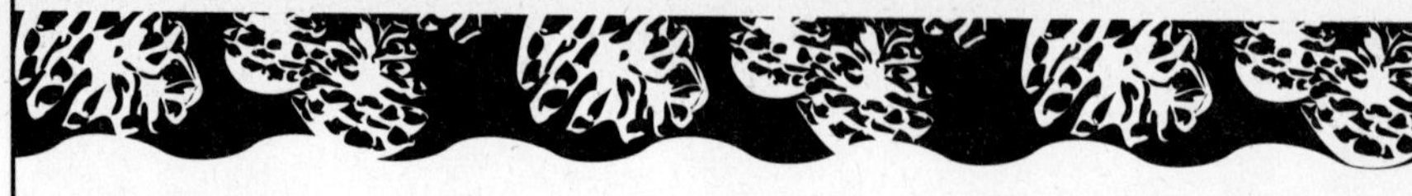

Name ______________________________

REFLECTION

6

What did Daniel gain from his experience in the mountains? What did the other boys gain?

____

____

____

____

____

____

Name ____________________

K-W-L Chart

Title ____________________

What I **K**now	What I **W**ant to Find Out	What I **L**earned

Name ______________________

My Notes to Clarify

Write any words or ideas that you need to clarify. Include the page numbers.

Words or Ideas	Page
Pages 8–13	
Pages 14–17	
Pages 18–21	
Pages 22–26	
Pages 27–32	
Pages 33–37	
Pages 38–45	

There's a Wolf in the Classroom

Name ______________________________

REFLECTION 1

Do you think it was a good idea for Bruce and Pat to raise a wolf? Why?

____

____

____

____

____

REFLECTION 2

Do you think Pat and Bruce are taking good care of Koani? Explain your opinion.

____

____

____

____

____

____

Name ____________________

REFLECTION

3

Which strategies have you used while reading *There's a Wolf in the Classroom*?

____

Explain how and why each strategy helped you.

Predict

____

____

____

Question

____

____

____

Clarify

____

____

____

Summarize

____

____

____

Name ______________________________

REFLECTION

4

Summarize what you learned about wolf behavior on pages 22–26.

____

____

____

____

____

____

REFLECTION

5

Explain why wolves don't make good pets.

____

____

____

____

Name ______________________

REFLECTION

6

Do you think Koani will be a good teacher? Why or why not?

REFLECTION

7

What were some of the most important and interesting facts you learned about wolves from this book?

Name ______________________________

Story Map

Title

Setting

Characters

Problem

Major Events

Outcome

Name ______________________________

My Notes to Clarify

Write any words or ideas that you need to clarify. Include the page numbers.

Words or Ideas	Page
Pages 1–17	
Pages 18–32	
Pages 33–49	
Pages 50–64	
Pages 65–79	
Pages 80–84	

Name ______________________________

REFLECTION **1**

Why is having money so important to Sarah Ida?

REFLECTION **2**

Do you think Aunt Claudia is being fair to Sarah Ida?
Why or why not?

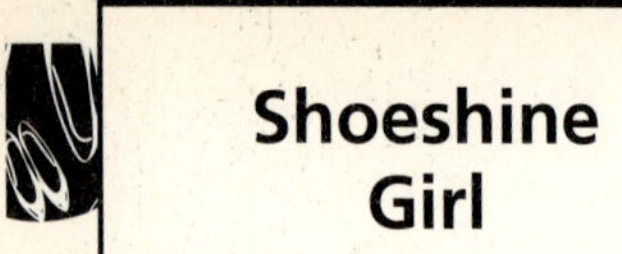

Name ______________________________

REFLECTION

3

If you were one of Sarah Ida's customers, what would you say to her about expecting tips?

____

____

____

REFLECTION

4

Why do you think the medal is so special to Al?

____

____

____

____

Shoeshine Girl

Name ______________________________

Circle one strategy that helped you to read *Shoeshine Girl.*

Strategy Box			
Predict	**Summarize**	**Clarify**	**Question**

Explain how you used that strategy.

____

____

____

____

Name ______________________

REFLECTION 6

What do Sarah Ida and Al learn about each other?

How is Sarah Ida different at the end of the story than she was at the beginning?

Name ____________________

K-W-L Chart

Title

What I Know	What I Want to Find Out	What I Learned

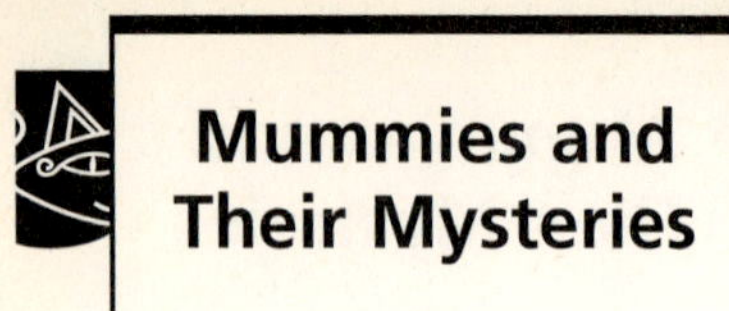

Name ____________________

My Notes to Clarify

Write any words or ideas that you need to clarify. Include the page numbers.

Words or Ideas	Page
Pages 6–14	
Pages 15–22	
Pages 23–27	
Pages 28–36	
Pages 37–45	
Pages 46–55	
Pages 56–59	

Name ____________________

REFLECTION

1 How could an animal become a mummy naturally?

REFLECTION

2 Summarize what Egyptians did to provide "houses" for spirits of the dead.

Name ______________________________

REFLECTION

Circle the section you liked best so far in *Mummies and Their Mysteries.*

Pages 6–14	Pages 15–22	Pages 23–27
What Is a Mummy?	**The Most Famous Mummies—Egypt**	**Millions of Mummies—the Incan Empire**

How did one or more of the four strategies help you read that section?

Predict

____

____

Summarize

____

____

Clarify

____

____

Question

____

____

____

Name ______________________________

REFLECTION

4

What beliefs about death did the Anasazi share with most mummy makers?

REFLECTION

5

What did scientists learn from studying the mummies of explorers?

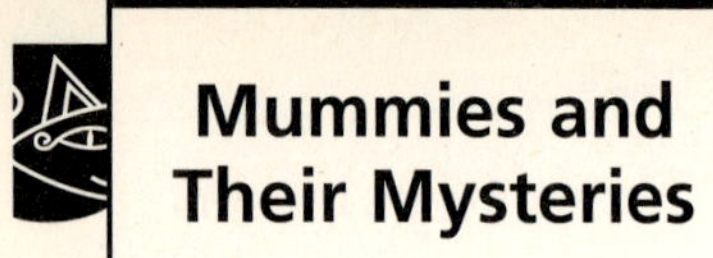

Mummies and Their Mysteries

Name ______________________

REFLECTION

6

Why do you think that people were thrown into a bog after a violent death?

REFLECTION

7

If you saw a mummy in a museum, what would you know about it?

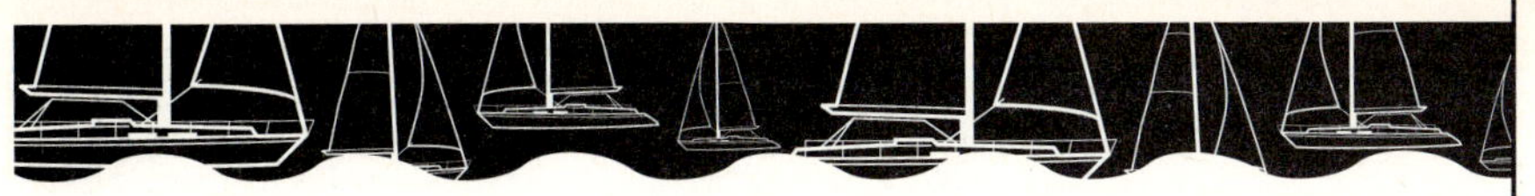

Windcatcher

Name ______________________________

Story Map

Title

Setting

Characters

Problem

Major Events

Outcome

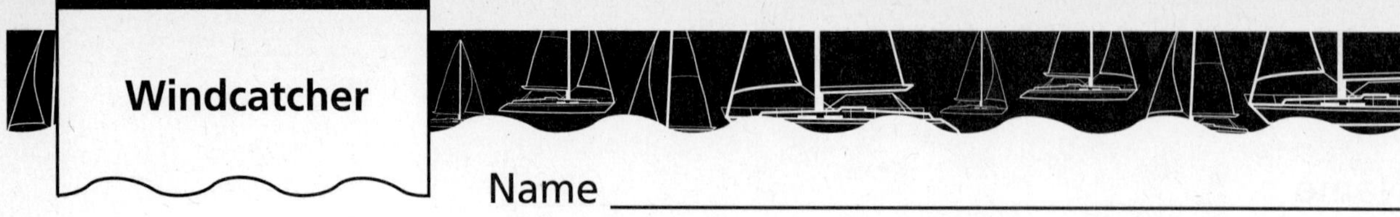

Name ______________________

My Notes to Clarify

Write any words or ideas that you need to clarify. Include the page numbers.

Words or Ideas	Page
Pages 1–20	
Pages 21–38	
Pages 39–51	
Pages 52–69	
Pages 70–87	
Pages 88–109	
Pages 110–124	

Name ______________________________

REFLECTION

1

Why is buying a sailboat so important to Tony?

____

____

____

____

____

____

REFLECTION

2

Do you think Tony will learn to be a good sailor?
Why or why not?

____

____

____

____

____

____

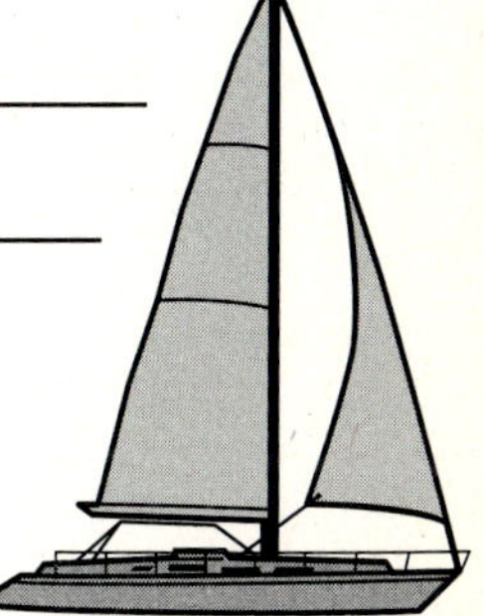

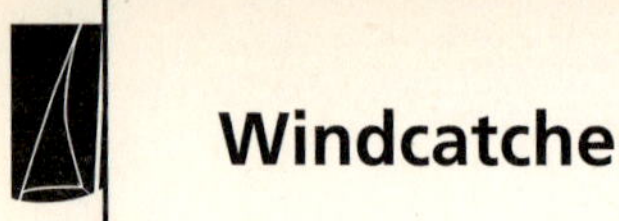

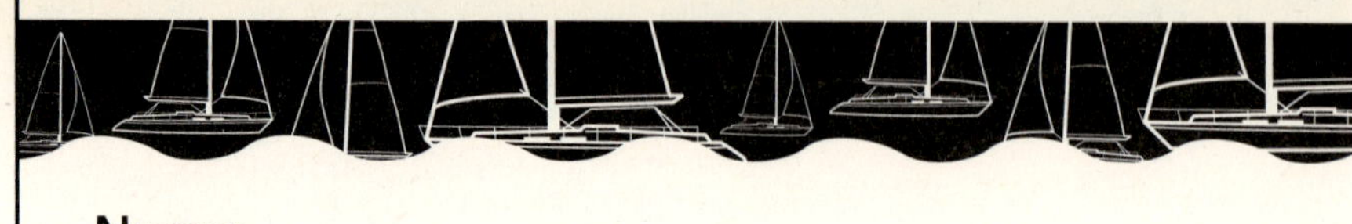

Name ____________________

REFLECTION

3

Do you think Tony is ready to sail by himself?
Why or why not?

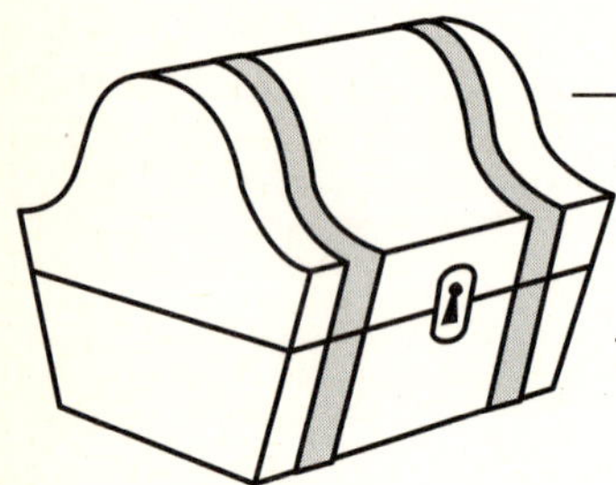

REFLECTION

4

Why do you think the man tells Tony to keep away from their motorboat?

Name ____________________

Which strategy has helped you most so far in reading *Windcatcher?*

Strategy Box			
Predict	**Summarize**	**Clarify**	**Question**

Explain how that strategy helped you.

____

____

____

____

____

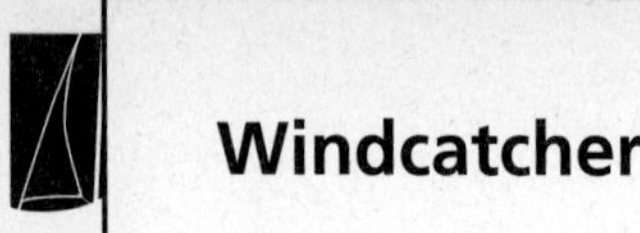

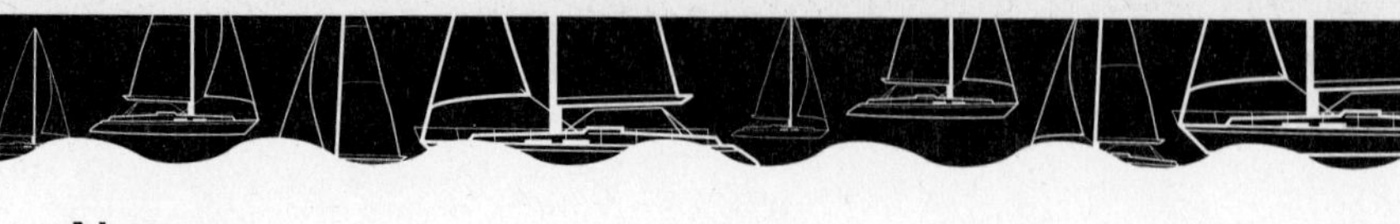

Name ____________________

REFLECTION

6

Do you think it is a good idea for Tony to swim the channel? Why or why not?

REFLECTION

7

What do you think Tony learns about doing things on his own?

Clarify/Phonics How to Say a Word

When I come to a word I don't know, first I look for chunks I know. I know ________. If I still don't know the word, I look for letter sounds. In this word, I know the sounds ____, ____, and ____. If I blend the sounds together, the word is ____________________. Finally, I check the meaning by rereading the sentence.

Clarify A Word Meaning

I read this word: ____________________. I'm not sure what this word is or what it means. I look at the picture or read to the end of the sentence. Now I think the word means . . .

Clarify An Idea

I don't understand this idea: ____________________.

First I ____________________ (reread, look at pictures, etc.). Then I understand that . . . I reread the sentence and it makes sense.

Predict

When I predict, I use clues from the pictures or from what I have read to help me figure out what will happen next (or what I will learn). I predict . . .

Question

When I question, I ask something that can be answered as I read or after I finish reading. I might ask . . .

Summarize

When I summarize, I tell in my own words the important things I have read.

Name ___________________________

Book Log

Title	Author	Date Completed	Comments

Name ______________________________

Book Log

Title	Author	Date Completed	Comments